BY JONAH WINTER

ILLUSTRATED BY SEAN QUALLS

Arthur A. Levine Books • An Imprint of Scholastic Inc.

LIBRARY OF CONGRESS CATALOGING-IN-PUBLICATION DATA

Winter, Jonah.
Dizzy / by Jonah Winter; illustrated by Sean Qualls. p. cm.
ISBN 0-439-50737-5
1. Gillespie, Dizzy, 1917–Juvenile literature. 2. Jazz musicians–United States–Biography–Juvenile literature.
I. Qualls, Sean, ill. II. Title. ML3930.G47W56 2006   788.9'2165092–dc22 2005024043

10 9 8 7 6 5 4 3   07 08 09 10

First edition, October 2006
Printed in Singapore   46

Text type set in AG Book Rounded Bold. Display type set in AdLib BT.
The art for this book was created using acrylic paint, collage, and pencil.

Book design by Marijka Kostiw

For Marcello Carelli
J.W.

For my son, Isaiah
S.Q.

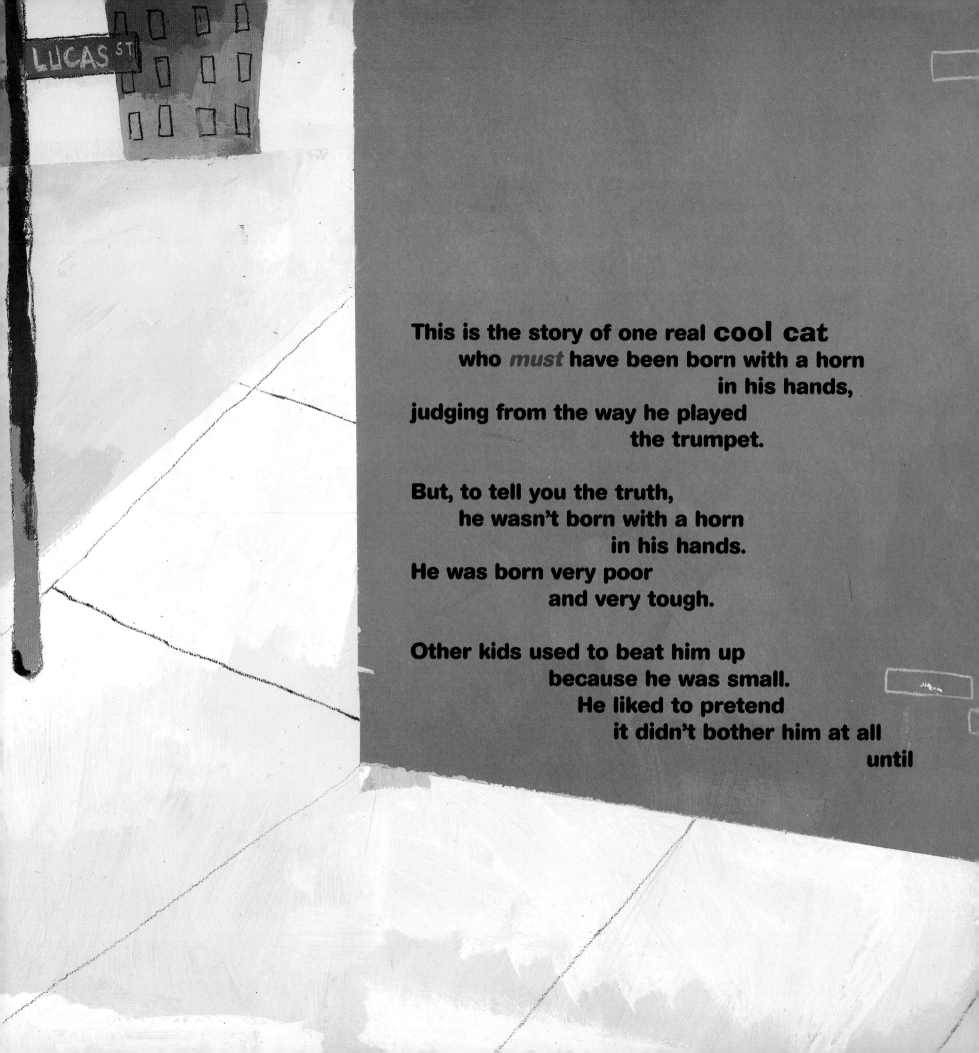

This is the story of one real cool cat
    who *must* have been born with a horn
                    in his hands,
judging from the way he played
                the trumpet.

But, to tell you the truth,
    he wasn't born with a horn
                in his hands.
He was born very poor
                and very tough.

Other kids used to beat him up
                because he was small.
                He liked to pretend
                    it didn't bother him at all
                                until

one day he just couldn't take it anymore.
He got mad
and he got even:
He whooped the living tar
out of some big bully

and before you knew it,
he was fighting all the time –
fighting and fighting
just for the sake of it.
There was no rhyme

nor reason to his fighting:

He was always mad.
You see, his dad
was always beating on HIM
and there was nothing he could do

but try to be tough
and try not to cry.

Then one day,
his music teacher gave him a trumpet.
He picked it up

and blew that thing as hard as he could.
That felt **GOOD!**
He took all the anger he felt inside
and blasted it out through the end of his horn.

IT WAS REALLY LOUD!

He didn't care how it sounded —
which was *pretty bad*
at first.
He just kept playing and playing,
day after day,

until he no longer felt the urge to fight.
His dad still whooped him,
but with every blow
he got from his dad,
he blew his trumpet that much more

until he was **ROARING.**
He was **SOARING.**
He was the best musician
in his little southern town —
soon that got boring.

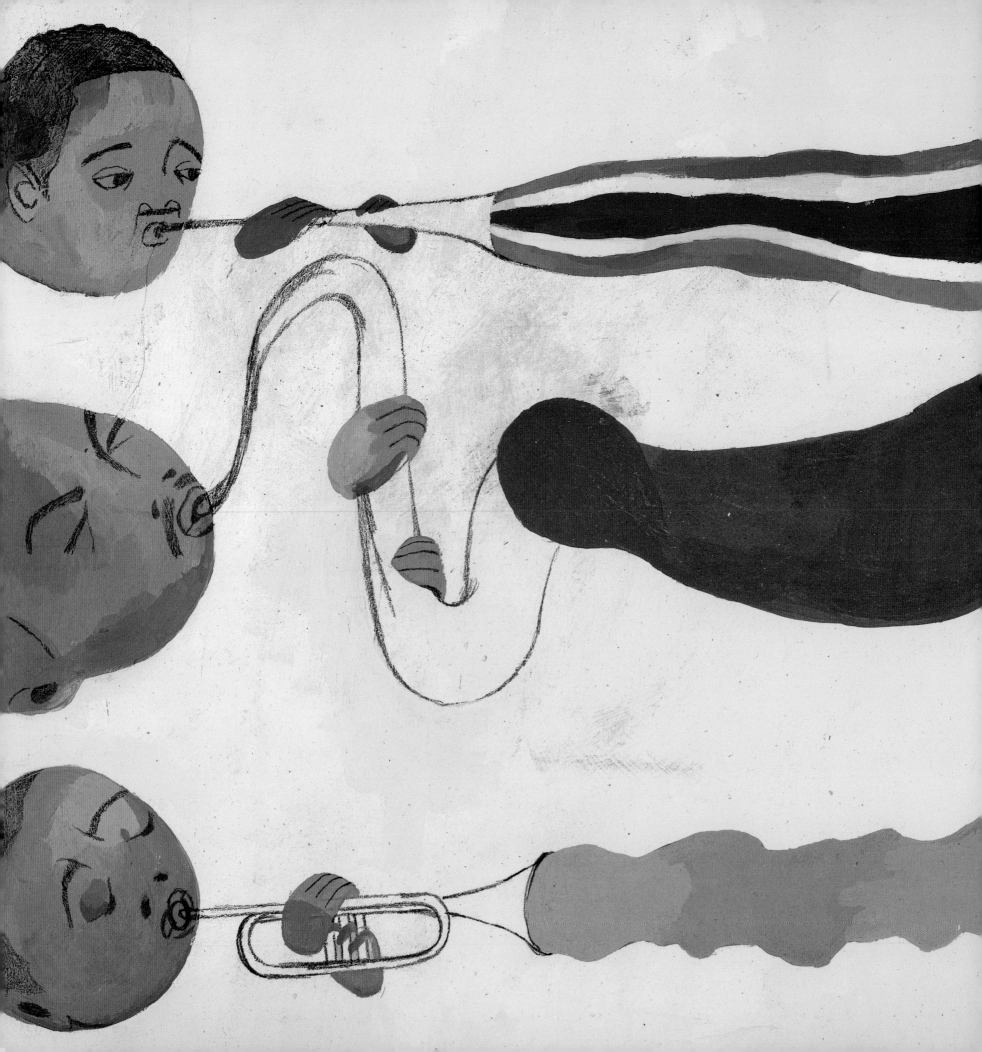

Playing notes on a page
was what he'd learned to do
but what he *wanted* to play
was a thing called *"jazz"* –

all over the radio, JAZZ
was the RAGE.

In JAZZ,
 you took a melody
 and played it all different ways.
You made up stuff
 and changed every phrase – it was   !

If a melody was like a *rule*,
 jazz was like *breaking the rules*,
 like inventing *new rules*.
 Jazz was like *getting in trouble* –
 it was FUN!

For the boy with the horn
fueled with a **FIRE**
that burned with every whooping,
JAZZ was like a *fire extinguisher.*
It was **cooooooool.**

For the boy with the horn, stuck
inside a Podunk town
in the Deep South, where white folks put you down,
JAZZ was also like a ticket
on a train to better days.

So he boarded that train and moved up north
to a place they call Philly.
Right off the bat,
he got a job in a jazz band
and started acting silly.

He'd fall off his chair,
kick his feet in the air,
flail around willy-nilly,
play practical jokes
on various folks.

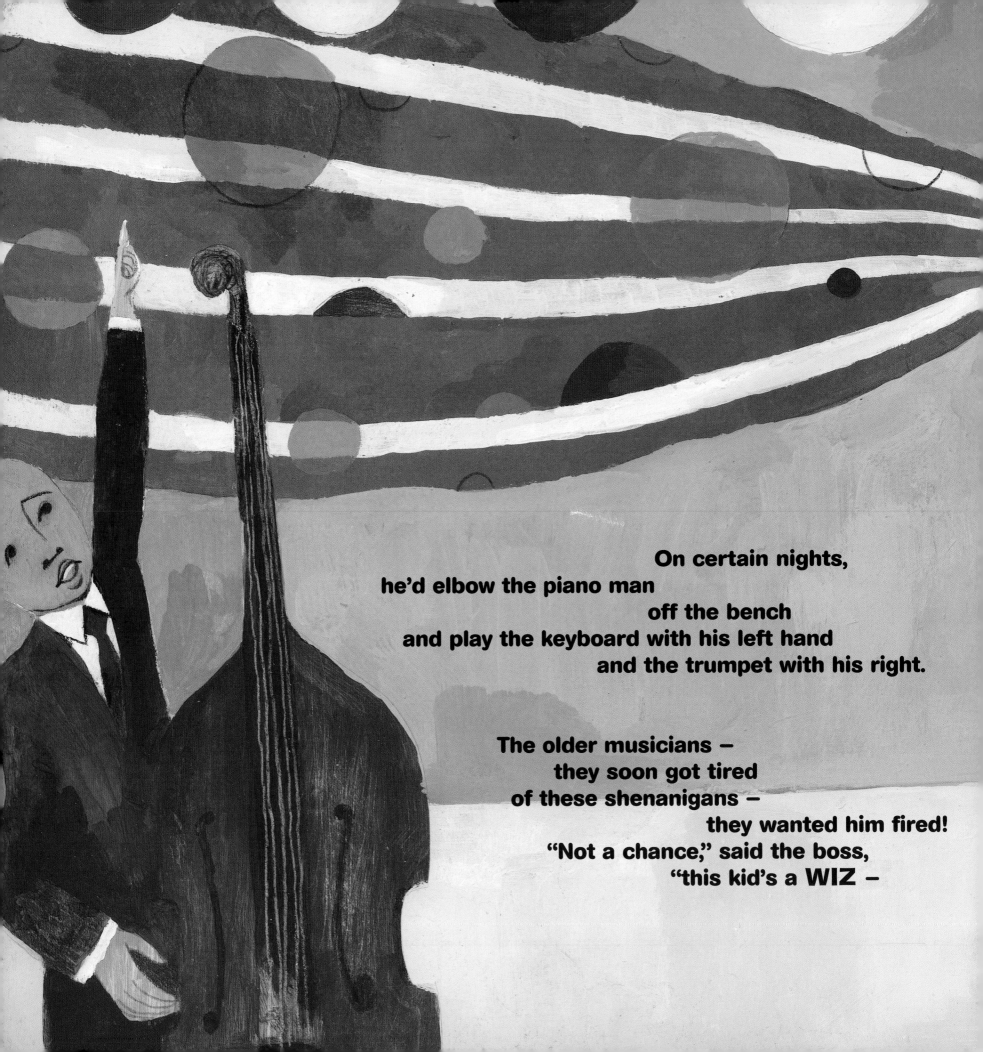

On certain nights,
he'd elbow the piano man
off the bench
and play the keyboard with his left hand
and the trumpet with his right.

The older musicians –
they soon got tired
of these shenanigans –
they wanted him fired!
"Not a chance," said the boss,
"this kid's a WIZ –

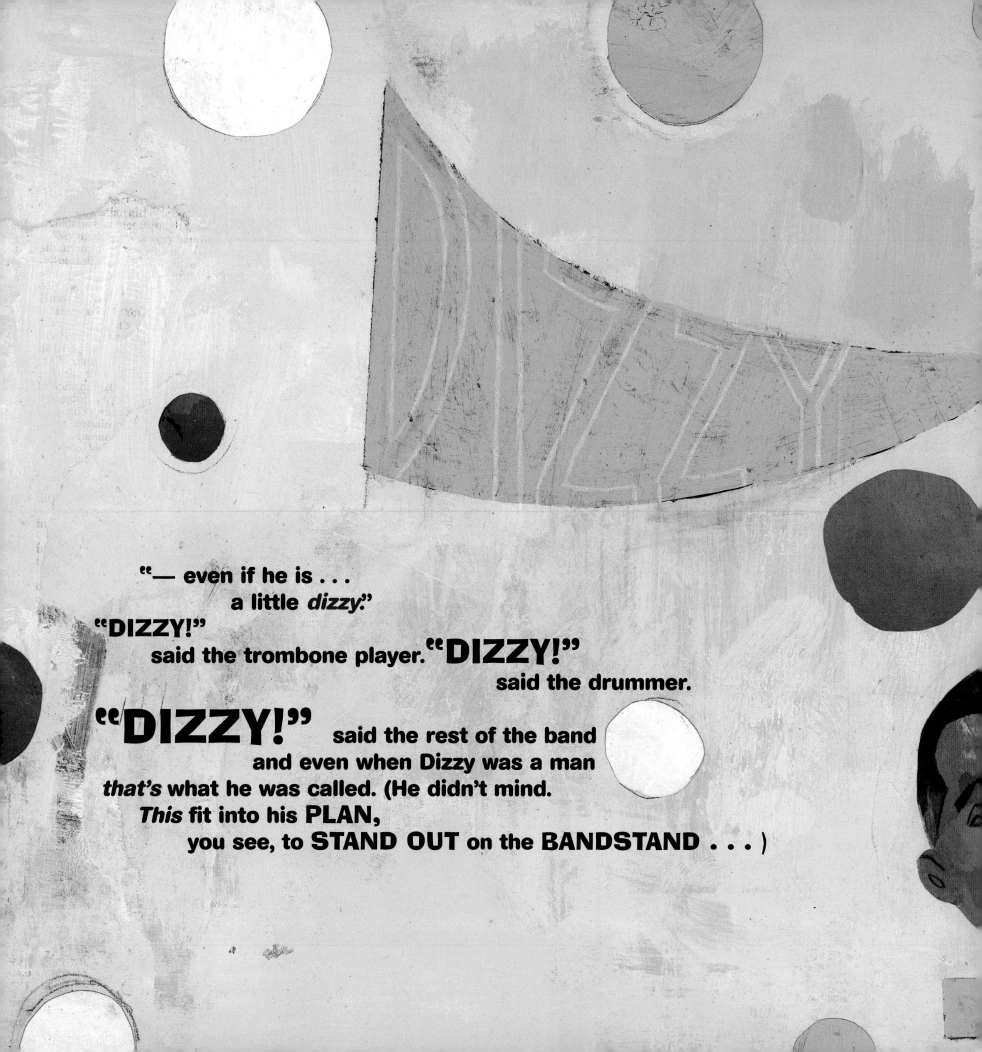

"— even if he is . . .
a little *dizzy*."
"DIZZY!"
said the trombone player. "DIZZY!"
said the drummer.

"DIZZY!"   said the rest of the band
and even when Dizzy was a man
that's what he was called. (He didn't mind.
This fit into his PLAN,
you see, to STAND OUT on the BANDSTAND . . .)

But Philly was SMALL TIME,
and Dizzy got bored,
so he caught the next train
to the town so nice, they named it twice:
NEW YORK, NEW YORK!

It was great!
What a place!
It was CRAZY
like jazz, sort of, like Dizzy himself,
except, *@&??##!$%*!! even crazier!
There were cars honking,
and everyone talking all at once
in different languages,
people laughing,
people shouting . . .

New York broke all the rules
just like Dizzy,
just like jazz.
It **NEVER** went to sleep —
people were up **ALL NIGHT** playing music

and dancing. And there was Dizzy,
horn beneath his arm,
soaking it in, the rumble and the roar
of the A train and the brass and the saxes and the drums
of the jazz clubs.

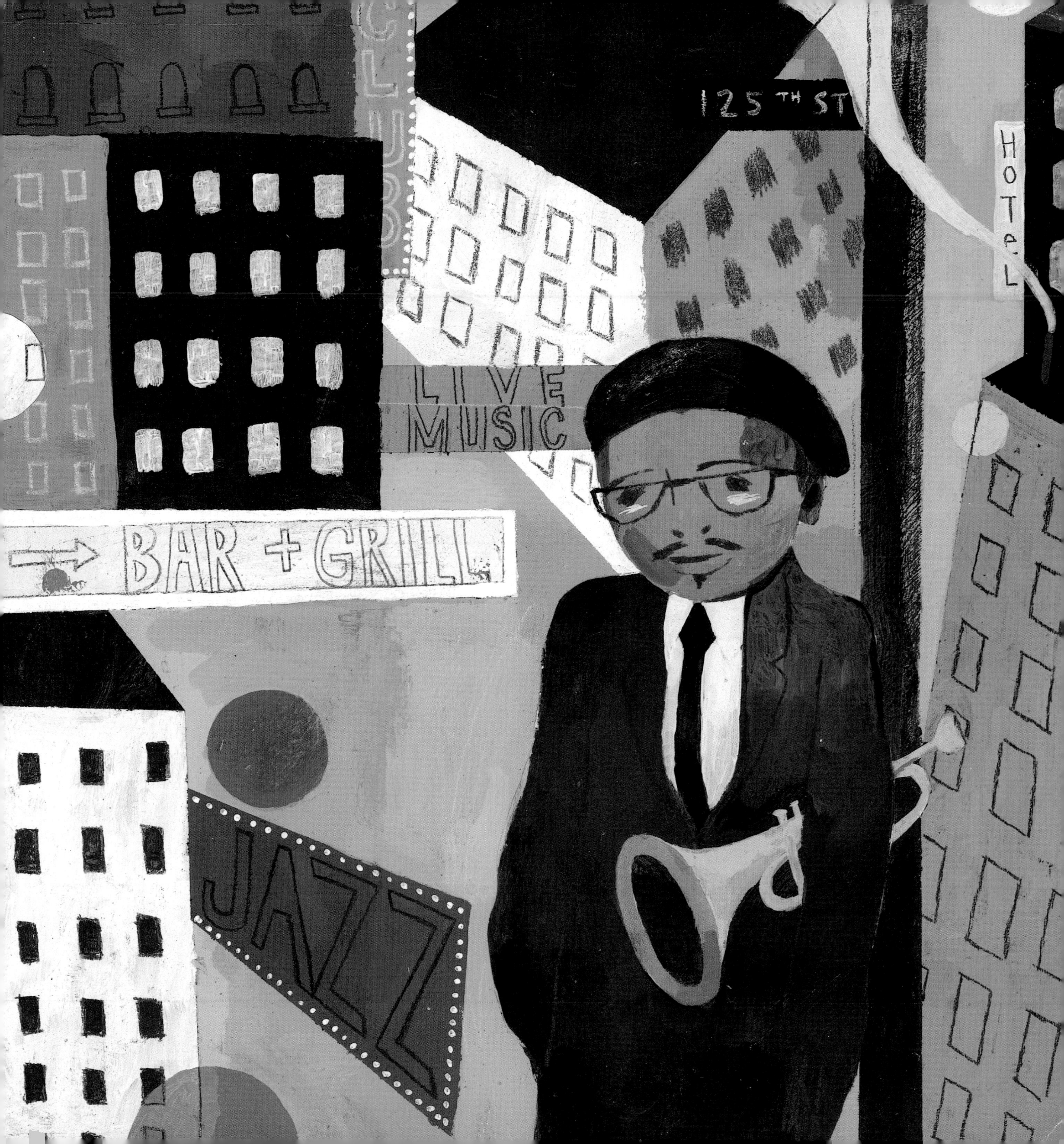

CLUB
125TH ST
HOTEL
LIVE MUSIC
BAR + GRILL
JAZZ

And there was Dizzy,
up onstage
with the **BEST JAZZ BAND** of them all!
Still, before long he was – *you guessed it* –
shooting spitballs
and clowning around,

making funny faces,
faking football passes
behind the back of the bandleader
while the **DUDE** was trying to **SING**,
PARTLY to get a laugh, but **MAINLY**
to get **NOTICED**.

You see,
Dizzy knew he'd have to do something *really*
special to get noticed in **THIS** band.
That's why, when it was Dizzy's turn
to stand up and play,
he played *WEIRD*-sounding notes:

He played so high,

he played so low,

he played so fast,

he played *diddly diddly bop de biddly wah wah de* **BLEEEEP,**

he puffed his cheeks out like this.

During breaks and after the show,
Dizzy'd be up on the roof
  with some other *hepcats*,
  teaching them this and that, you know,
    how to play "dizzy,"
      how to play notes that no one had *used* yet . . .

Here's the thing:
Dizzy knew
that sooner or later
he was going to get fired for being a clown
but he didn't care, because he was **PROUD**,

because somehow, somewhere, the man they called **DIZZY**
had come up with some not-so-dizzy ideas
on how to **CHANGE** jazz into something **NEW**,

and after he lost his job –

(OOP BOP SH'BAM!) –

like a preacher he spread the word
of his new jazz rhythms and chords
in late-night sessions and late-night clubs,
where folks would sit – NOT DANCE –
and listen, just LISTEN

to the zeebidee BOP – zoo buoy dee BOP BOP

ziddly BEEP

ziddly BOP

dee-BLAP   dee-BLOP

zee boot-n-dee bop'm dee bop'm dee BOP.

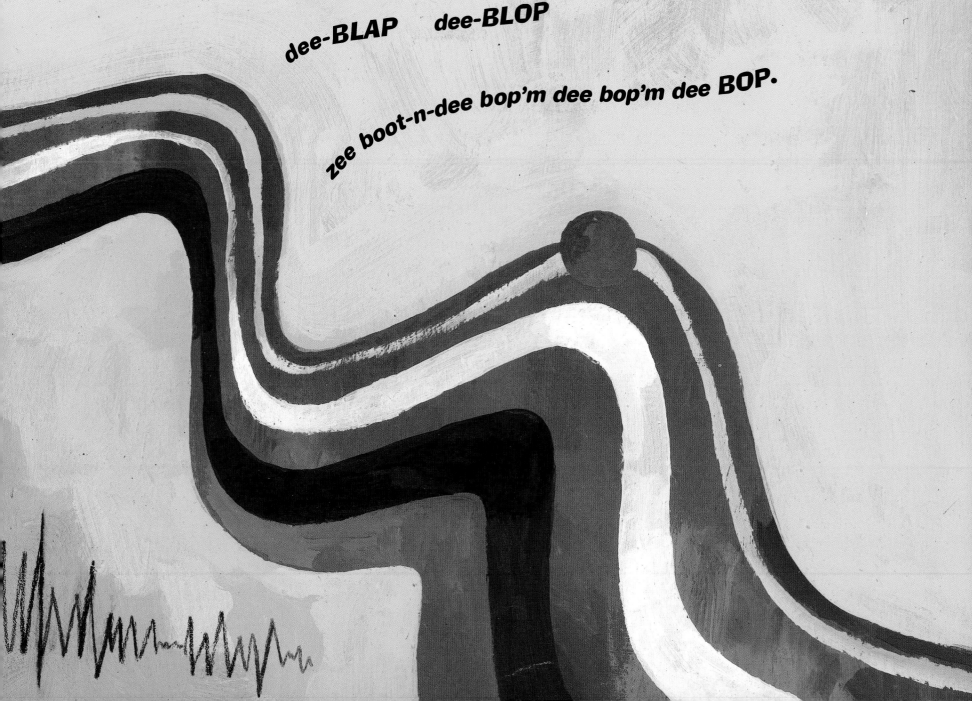

TONIGHT

DIZZY GILLESPIE

It was like he had taken a wrecking ball
and **SMASHED IN**
The House of Jazz,
till the walls came tumbling down,
and in its place

he built a new house, *The House of Coooooool Jazzzzzzzzzzzzz.*

Soon his *whole name* was up in big letters
on the sign outside:
DIZZY GILLESPIE

DIZZY GILLESPIE
on top of the world
going going going *ziddly dee-boo-dah-boo*
hiddly on his horn,   and then,
if he ran out of notes, he'd say:

"BEBOP."

That's what Dizzy called
this **CRAZY** kind of jazz
that he had invented just
by having the courage to be himself

until the *very thing* that had gotten him into trouble
                                            so much –
                        being a clown, breaking all the rules –
had become the thing that made him great,
                                            his ticket

            into Jazz Heaven
where, on certain nights,
Dizzy Gillespie
still shoves the angel Gabriel out of the way
            and shows him how to play

Bebop

AUTHOR'S NOTE

John Birks "**Dizzy**" Gillespie was born in 1917, in the town of Cheraw, South Carolina. As a child, he fooled around on the piano from a very young age, and then picked up the trumpet when he was thirteen. Around this time, he also started listening to jazz on the radio and dreaming of someday becoming a jazz musician himself. The kind of jazz he listened to was called "swing," and it was played by big bands for people to dance to. When **Dizzy** moved up north, swing music was still pretty much the only kind of jazz that jazz musicians played, and so **Dizzy** joined a swing band and played it too. He was such a brilliant jazz trumpeter that he made it into one of the most famous bands in history, The Cab Calloway Orchestra. This was in 1939. It was around this time that he started getting bored with swing music and began concocting some of his own very far-out musical ideas. He tried them out in the Cab Calloway band, during his solos, which had a lot of notes, and didn't sound like anything anyone had ever played before. Sometimes he got lost in the middle of them and would just stop playing and start laughing. This clowning around got him fired, at which point he started writing his own tunes and playing them with small groups of other jazz musicians who were also bored with swing and playing for dances. The music he wrote and played with these musicians – including the great saxophonist Charlie Parker and brilliant pianist Thelonius Monk – was revolutionary, unlike anything that anyone had ever done. To many people's ears it sounded too complicated, too weird, not melodic enough – you couldn't dance to it. But by the 1950s, it had taken over jazz. It was, of course, called "bebop." **Dizzy Gillespie** not only invented bebop, he trained many of the young jazz musicians of the 1940s, 50s, 60s, 70s, and 80s. Throughout his very full musical career, he was a great role model, not just musically, but in his personal life. Unlike many famous jazz musicians, he never used drugs *and* he was married to the same woman (Lorraine) his whole life. And up until his death in 1993, he proceeded through the world with a sense of fun and joy.